My Perfect Gift

_____

To

_____

From

_____

On this date

This book is dedicated to
my parents, James and Carol Dixon,
my offspring, Tyam, Max II,
and Christon (In Loving Memory)
their offspring Kingston, Kaiya, Mahari and Marli,
and the generations to come.
~Kingdom Family Legacy

Listen, O my people, to my teaching;

Incline your ears to the words of my mouth [and be willing to learn].

I will open my mouth in a parable [to instruct using examples];

I will utter dark and puzzling sayings of old [that contain important truth]

Which we have heard and known,

And our fathers have told us.

We will not hide them from their children,

But [we will] tell to the generation to come the praiseworthy deeds of the LORD,

And [tell of] His great might and power and the wonderful works that He has done.

For He established a testimony (a specific precept) in Jacob

And appointed a law in Israel,

Which He commanded our fathers

That they should teach to their children [the great facts of God's transactions with Israel],

That the generation to come might know them, that the children still to be born may arise

and retell them to their children, that they should place their confidence (trust) in God

And not forget the works of God,

But keep His commandments,

~Psalm 78:1-7

'Twas the Night Christ was Born

By Tonya Bozeman-Dixon

Illustrated By
Wulan Hastungkara

'Twas the night Christ was born in Bethlehem town.
Many traveled the roads climbing hills up and down.

NO ROOM

They were going to be counted and pay taxes too.
Caesar said this is what they all had to do.

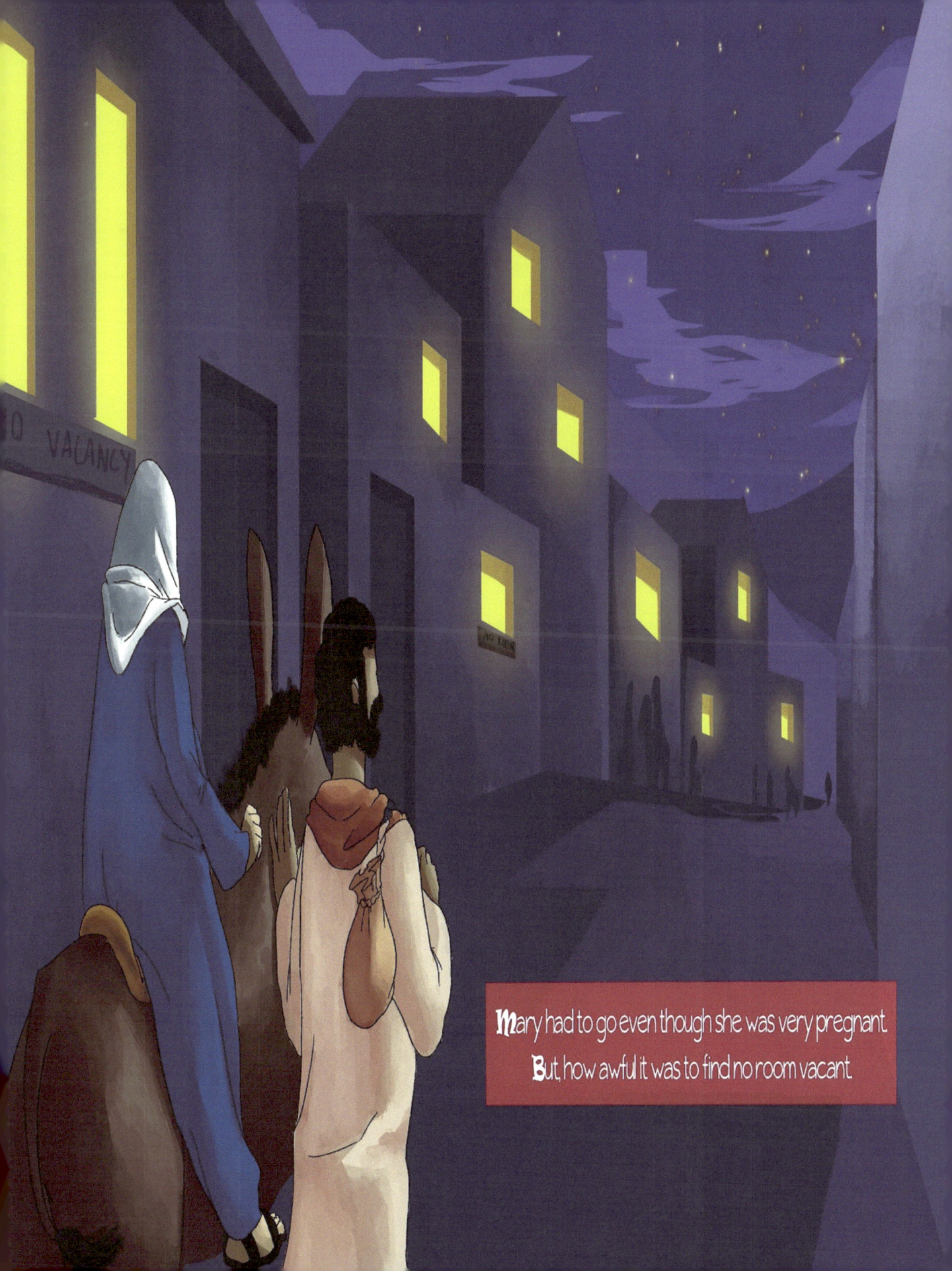

Mary had to go even though she was very pregnant.
But, how awful it was to find no room vacant.

They were very, very tired and wanted a place to lay their heads.
When the innkeeper said, "I'm sorry I have no bed."

NO
VACAN

"But, I do have a place where you might get some rest.
I see her condition however, it's my best."

They followed him out to his animal stable.
But, they didn't complain it was the only thing available.

Joseph fluffed up the hay to make Mary as comfortable as can be, when all of a sudden she cried, "Oh the baby!"

Joseph replied, "Mary this can't be the time." But it was exactly what God had in mind.

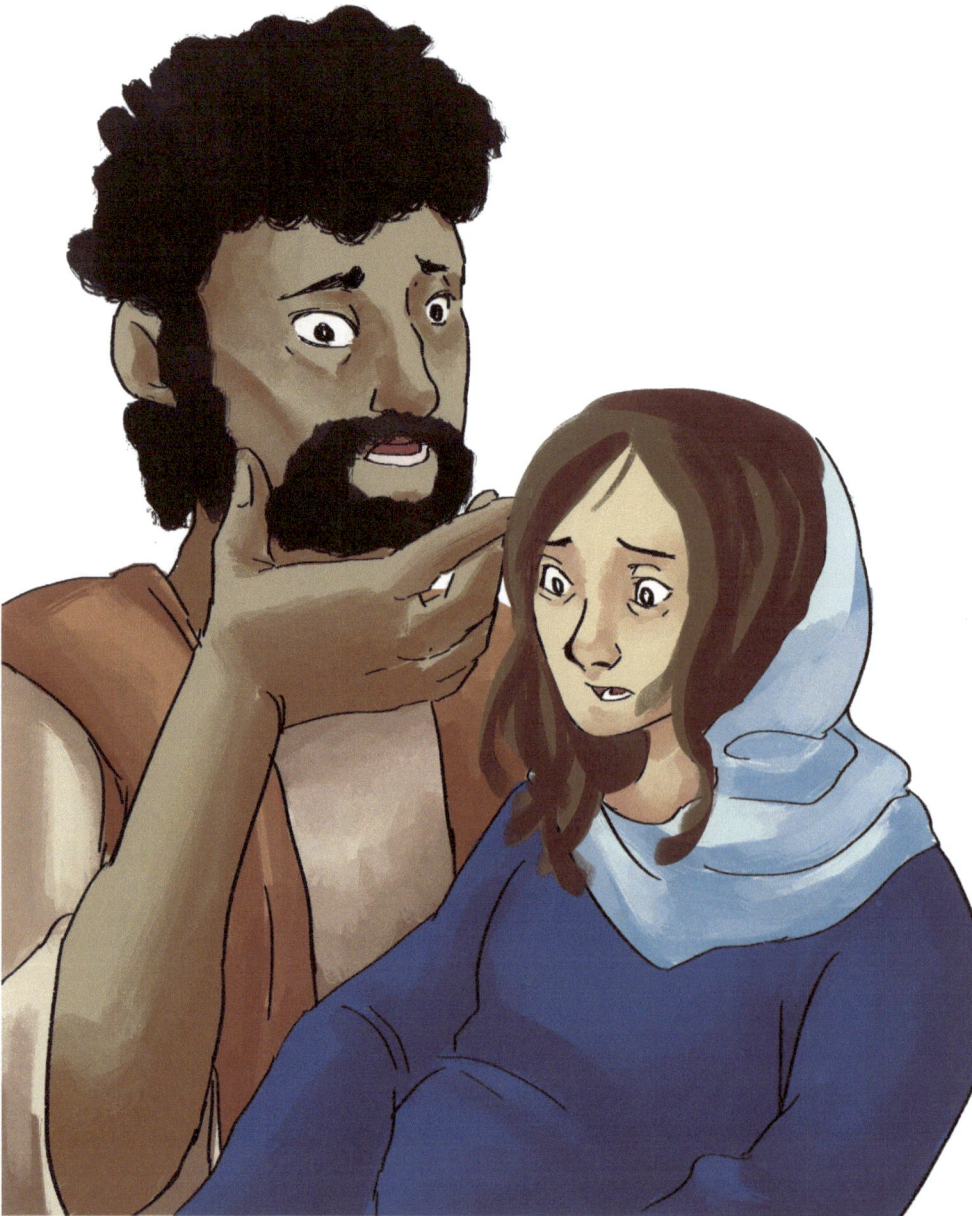

God's son who is King, born in a stable meek and low,
came to bring a message of love and salvation to even the poor.

Jesus was born and in a manger laid,

What a hard bed for a new born babe.

The Lord himself will give you a sign and the virgin will conceive and give birth to a son. He will be called Immanuel, which means "God with us!"

Isaiah 7:14 NIV Revised

"The virgin will give birth to a son and you are to name him Jesus, because he will save his people from their sins."

Matthew 1:21

The angels announced Jesus' birth, singing Glory to God and Peace on Earth!

Wisemen came from near and far guided by a brightly, shining star.

The wise men traveling saw the star in the east. They went to place gifts at Jesus' feet.

They had heard of the Savior that was to come,

And immediately recognized he was the Holy One!

For unto us [each of us] a child is born,
to us a son is given and the government
[sin penalty] will be on his
shoulders.
And he will be called Wonderful Counselor, Mighty God,
Everlasting Father, Prince of Peace.

Isaiah 9:6 Revised

The news traveled fast that the King
was born.

Just like the prophet had written
to forewarn.

The news of Jesus' birth made King Herod and his friends upset.
Being the king of the land, Herod saw King Jesus as a threat.

An angel came to Joseph has they lay fast asleep.

Told him, "Get up, go to Egypt. I want you to flee!"

Yes, 'Twas the night Christ was born,
God began His plan,

That would link us to Him
Hand in Hand!

"For God so [greatly] loved the world [all the people]
so much that He [even] gave His [One and] only begotten Son,
so that whoever believes and trusts in Him [as Savior]
shall not perish, but have eternal life [live forever with Him]."

John 3:16 AMPV Revised

I'm Thankful!

(Draw or attach a picture of yourself)

Dear God,
I thank you for loving me so much that you proved it by allowing your only son, Jesus to leave you in Heaven, be born through Mary and to Joseph and give His life to save me from the punishment of my sins [wrong doings] through his death and resurrection. In Jesus' name I pray, amen.

Thanksgiving Prayer

Thank you Lord for a chance to pray,
Thank you for keeping us until this day

Thank you for our daily bread,
And a place to lay our heads

Thank you for your darling SON,
Thank you so much for ALL you've done.
In Jesus' name I pray, Amen.
~Tonya Bozeman-Dixon

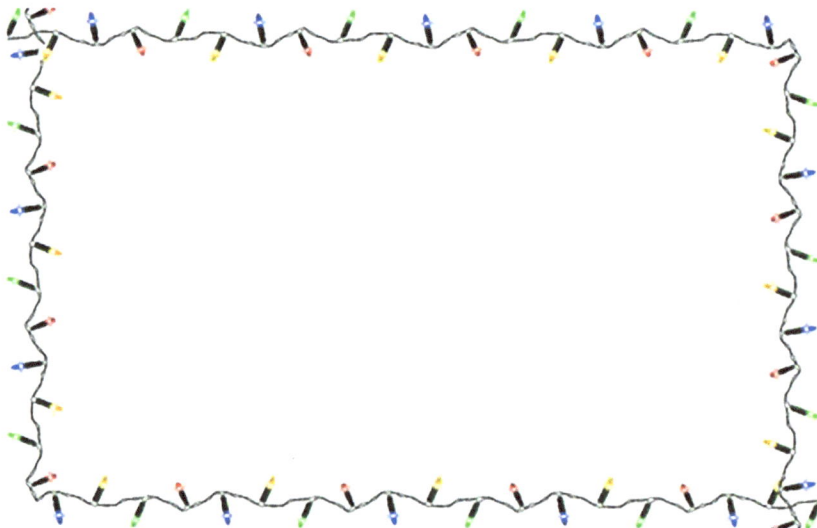

(Draw or attach a picture of your family)

ISBN 978-0-692-99441-2

First Book Shelf Edition, December 2017

'Twas the Night Christ was Born was inspired through the Biblical teachings and recordings of the Holy writings. The revision of noted verses derived from my interpretations of actual writings from the Holy Bible Gateway, NIV, AMP, NASB versions.

To order additional copies of this book, the MP4 version, or the MP3 Read-a-long:
Please visit www.twasthenightchristwasborn.com or visit Amazon.com or your local bookstore.

For special appearances, storytelling, or other products and services please contact:
It'z a Kidz Thing at itsakidzthing@yahoo.com

Acknowledgments

"The existence of a burning candle is to give of itself through the melting of its wax through the heated fire, allowing its existence to diminish for the benefit of providing the source of light to others."   ~Tonya Bozeman-Dixon

To My Candles...

James and Carrol Dixon, Parents

"Your life-long lessons of devotion, discipline, and dedication to God, people and service is what directs my path and drives me to be determined to achieve all and be all to God's Glory!"

Bishop James Dixon, II, Brother and Pastor

"God spoke to you concerning me. You exemplified your faith in Him, to be at work in me, by entrusting me to care for your most tender sheep he placed in your care. Thank you for allowing me to hang around you as your little sister, caring and watching over me, and always having a word of wisdom to share. As you became my Spiritual Father, these attributes became even more valued and appreciated. You taught me that when our physical walk here on earth comes to an end we will continue our spiritual journey, eternal in the heavens."

Timothy and Carlondria Dixon, Siblings

"There are times I have to convince myself that you all are not omnipresent because no matter what I'm doing you're always supporting and cheering my on to victory!" Your prayers, words of encouragement and unwavering love and support are embellishments for all I do."

Tyam Richard and Max Bozeman, II, Offspring

"Life with you has yielded much increase to me. In any attempt to calculate what I may have given to you, my calculations always comes up far less than what you've given to me through the multiplied dividends of your love, honor, respect, and hope for our future."

Christon Bozeman, Offspring (In Loving Memory)

"I've always said, 'you were my poster child' because the life experiences encountered with you have served as my training field for the children and parents God has willed to me to minister to. Every lesson of love, grace, loyalty, and hope will be cherished forever!"
Love, Hugs and Kisses

The Creative, Technical and Support Team

"Each one needs one and boy did I need each of you! Each of you delivered a stellar performance in the editing process, creation of illustrations, typing setting, production, distribution and marketing. Your encouragement, demonstration of faith in this project and certainly your prayers are more cherished than a treasure chest of precious gems." To a special gem, *Christie Steverson*, your worth-ship to me and this project are priceless!

www.ingramcontent.com/pod-product-compliance
Lightning Source LLC
LaVergne TN
LVHW072101070426
835508LV00002B/204